HAVE YOURS[ELF]

A Merry Christmas

MW00800941

Editor: Carol Cuellar

Cover Photo: Copyright © 1994 FPG International,
Monserrate Schwartz

CONTENTS

CHRISTMAS EVE IN MY HOME TOWN

Words and Music by
STAN ZABKA and
DON UPTON

Christmas Eve In My Home Town - 3 - 1

4

can't help rem - i - nisc - ing, know - ing I'll be miss - ing

CHRIST - MAS EVE IN MY HOME TOWN. Noth - ing can e - rase

mem - 'ries I em - brace __ those fa - mil - iar foot - prints up - on the snow! ___ There's

so much to re - mem - ber! No won - der I re - mem - ber

CHRIST - MAS EVE IN MY HOME TOWN. I'd like to be there,

THE BELLS OF CHRISTMAS
(HEAR THE BELLS)

Words and Music by
MARY STUART

The Bells Of Christmas - 2 - 1

CHRISTMAS LULLABY

Lyric by
PEGGY LEE

Music by
CY COLEMAN

GOD REST YE MERRY, GENTLEMEN

TRADITIONAL

God Rest Ye Merry Gendemen - 2 - 1

ti - dings of com - fort and joy, com-fort and

joy, o _____ ti - dings of com - fort and joy.

3. In Bethlehem, in Jewry
   This blessed Babe was born,
   And laid within a manger
   Upon this holy morn,
   The which his Mother Mary
   Did nothing take in scorn.
   　　O tidings, etc.

4. "Fear not then," said the Angel,
   "Let nothing you affright,
   This day is born a Saviour
   Of a pure Virgin bright,
   To free all those who trust in Him
   From Satan's power and might."
   　　O tidings, etc.

5. The shepherds at those tidings
   Rejoiced much in mind,
   And left their flocks a-feeding,
   In tempest, storm, and wind:
   And went to Bethlehem straightway,
   The Song of God to find.
   　　O tidings, etc.

6. And when they came to Bethlehem
   Where our dear Saviour lay,
   They found Him in a manger,
   Where oxen feed on hay;
   His Mother Mary kneeling down,
   Unto the Lord did pray.
   　　O tidings, etc.

7. Now to the Lord sing praises,
   All you within this place,
   And with true love and brotherhood
   Each other now embrace;
   This holy tide of Christmas
   All other doth deface.
   　　O tidings, etc.

God Rest Ye Merry Gentlemen - 2 - 2

THE FIRST NOEL

TRADITIONAL

GOOD KING WENCESLAS

TRADITIONAL

2. "Hither, page, and stand by me,
   If thou know'st it telling,
   Yonder peasant, who is he?
   Where and what his dwelling?"
   "Sire, he lives a good league hence,
   Underneath the mountain,
   Right against the forest fence,
   By St. Agnes' fountain."

3. "Bring me flesh, and bring me wine,
   Bring me pine logs hither;
   Thou and I will see him dine,
   When we bear them thither."
   Page and monarch, forth they went,
   Forth they went together;
   Through the rude wind's wild lament,
   And the bitter weather.

4. "Sire, the night is darker now,
   And the wind blows stronger;
   Fails my heart, I know not how;
   I can go no longer."
   "Mark my footsteps my good page,
   Tread thou in them boldly:
   Thou shalt find the winter's rage
   Freeze thy blood less coldly."

5. In his master's steps he trod,
   Where the snow lay dinted;
   Heat was in the very sod
   Which the Saint had printed.
   Therefore, Christian men, be sure,
   Wealth or rank possessing,
   Ye who now will bless the poor,
   Shall yourselves find blessing.

A GREAT AND MIGHTY WONDER

GERMAN

A Great And Mighty Wonder - 2 - 1

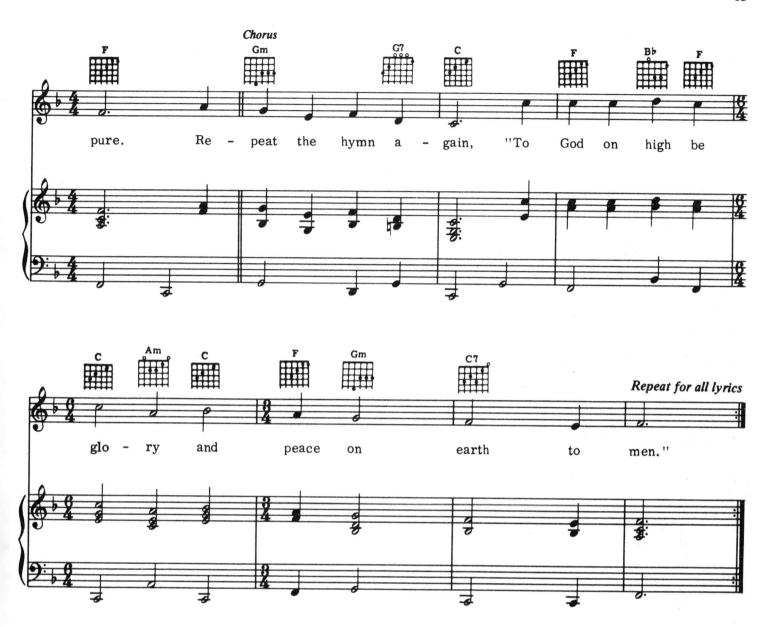

Chorus

pure. Re - peat the hymn a - gain, "To God on high be

Repeat for all lyrics

glo - ry and peace on earth to men."

2. The Word becomes incarnate
   And yet remains on high!
   And cherubim sing anthems
   To shepherds from the sky.

3. While thus they sing your Monarch,
   Those bright angelic bands
   Rejoice, ye vales and mountains,
   Ye oceans, clap your hands.

4. Since all He comes to ransom,
   By all be He adorned,
   The infant born in Bethl'em,
   The Saviour and the Lord.

5. And idol forms shall perish,
   And error shall decay,
   And Christ shall wield His sceptre,
   Our Lord and God for aye.

HARK! THE HERALD ANGELS SING

Words and Music by
FELIX MENDELSSOHN
and CHAS. WESLEY

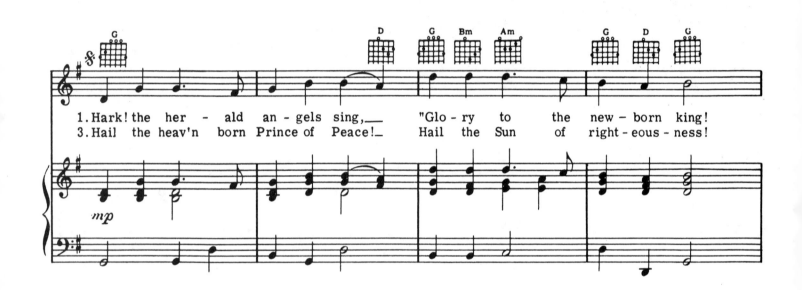

1. Hark! the her - ald an - gels sing,___ "Glo - ry to the new - born king!
3. Hail the heav'n born Prince of Peace!___ Hail the Sun of right - eous - ness!

Peace on earth and mer - cy mild;___ God and sin - ners re - con - ciled."
Light and life to all He brings,___ Ris'n with heal - ing in His wings.

Hark! the Herald Angels Sing - 3 - 1

HAVE YOURSELF A MERRY LITTLE CHRISTMAS

Words and Music by
HUGH MARTIN and
RALPH BLANE

Have Yourself a Merry Little Christmas - 3 - 1

HERE COMES SANTA CLAUS
(Right Down Santa Claus Lane)

Words and Music by
GENE AUTRY and
OAKLEY HALDEMAN

THE HOLLY AND THE IVY

TRADITIONAL

2. The holly bears a blossom,
   As white as lily flow'r,
   And Mary bore sweet Jesus Christ,
   To be our sweet Saviour.

   Refrain

3. The holly bears a berry,
   As red as any blood,
   And Mary bore sweet Jesus Christ,
   To do poor sinners good.

   Refrain

From the Videocraft T.V. Musical Spectacular "RUDOLPH THE RED-NOSED REINDEER"

A HOLLY JOLLY CHRISTMAS

By JOHNNY MARKS

A Holly Jolly Christmas - 2 - 1

A Holly Jolly Christmas - 2 - 2

I HEARD THE BELLS ON CHRISTMAS DAY

H. W. LONGFELLOW

HENRY BISHOP

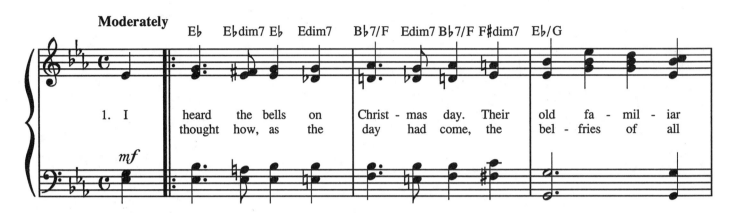

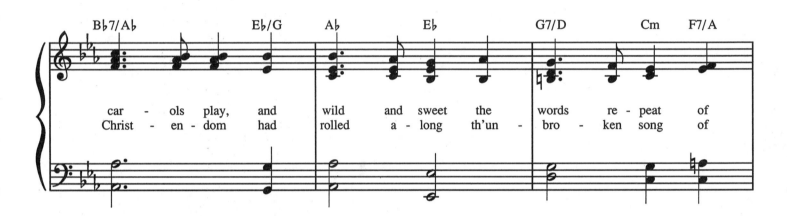

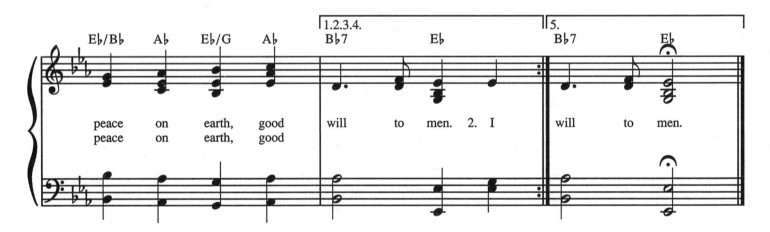

Verse 3:
And in despair I bowed my head:
"There is no peace on earth," I said,
"For hate is strong and mocks the song
Of peace on earth, good will to men."

Verse 4:
Then pealed the bells more loud and deep:
"God is not dead, nor doth He sleep;
The wrong shall fail, the right prevail,
With peace on earth, good will to men."

Verse 5:
Till, ringing, singing on its way,
The world revolv'd from night to day,
A voice, a chime, a chant sublime,
Of peace on earth, good will to men!

I WANT AN OLD-FASHIONED CHRISTMAS

Words by
FLORENCE TARR

Music by
FAY FOSTER

I Want An Old Fashioned Christmas - 3 - 1

28

I Want An Old Fashioned Christmas - 3 - 3

IT CAME UPON A MIDNIGHT CLEAR

Words by
EDMUND H. SEARS

Music by
RICHARD S. WILLIS

It Came Upon A Midnight Clear - 2 - 1

3. And ye beneath life's crushing load,
    Whose forms are bending low,
    Who toil along the climbing way
    With painful steps and slow,
    Look now! for glad and golden hours
    Come swiftly on the wing.
    O rest beside the weary road
    And hear the angels sing.

4. For lo, the days are hast'ning on,
    By prophet bards foretold,
    When with the ever circling years
    Comes round the age of gold,
    When peace shall over all the earth
    Its ancient splendor fling,
    And the whole world give back the song
    Which now the angels sing.

It Came Upon A Midnight Clear - 2 - 2

I'D LIKE TO TEACH THE WORLD TO SING
(In Perfect Harmony)

Words and Music by
B. BACKER, B. DAVIS,
R. COOK and R. GREENAWAY

I'd Like To Teach The World To Sing - 2 - 1

I'd Like To Teach The World To Sing - 2 - 2

I'LL BE HOME FOR CHRISTMAS

Lyric by KIM GANNON
Music by WALTER KENT

I'll Be Home For Christmas - 2 - 1

I'll Be Home For Christmas - 2 - 2

JINGLE BELLS

J. PIERPONT

Jingle Bells - 2 - 1

JOLLY OLD ST. NICHOLAS

TRADITIONAL

Jolly Old St. Nicholas - 2 - 1

Jolly Old St. Nicholas - 2 - 2

JOY TO THE WORLD

Words by ISAAC WATTS

Music by G.F. HANDEL

IT'S THE MOST WONDERFUL
TIME OF THE YEAR

By EDDIE POLA
and GEORGE WYLE

It's the Most Wonderful Time of the Year - 3 - 1

42

It's the Most Wonderful Time of the Year - 3 - 3

MERRY CHRISTMAS, DARLING

Lyric by FRANK POOLER

Music by RICHARD CARPENTER

Greet-ing cards have all been sent, the Christ-mas rush is through,

but I still have one wish to make, a spe-cial one for you:

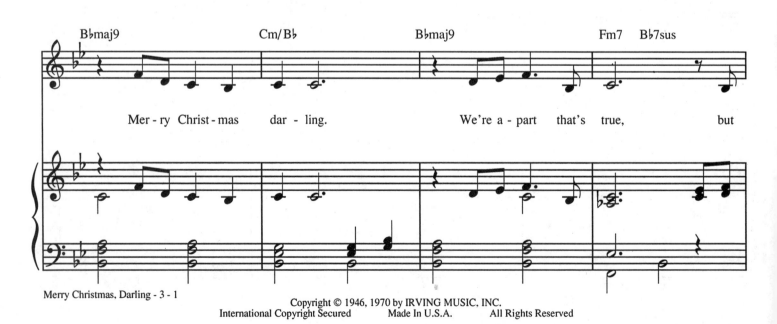

Mer - ry Christ-mas dar - ling. We're a - part that's true, but

Merry Christmas, Darling - 3 - 1

Merry Christmas, Darling - 3 - 2

O COME, ALL YE FAITHFUL
(Adeste Fideles)

JOHN READING

With great joy

Verse 2:
Sing, choirs of angels,
Sing in exultation,
Sing, all ye citizens of heaven above:
Glory to God
In the highest glory!
O come, let us adore Him, etc.

Verse 3:
Yea, Lord, we greet Thee,
Born this happy morning,
Jesus, to Thee be glory giv'n,
Word of the Father,
Now in flesh appearing.
O come, let us adore Him, etc.

THE NIGHT BEFORE CHRISTMAS SONG

Lyric adapted by
JOHNNY MARKS
From Clement Moore's Poem

Music by
JOHNNY MARKS

The Night Before Christmas Song - 2 - 1

O HOLY NIGHT
(Cantique de Noel)

By ADOLPH ADAM

O ho - ly night! The stars are bright - ly shin - ing. It is the night of our dear Sav - iour's birth. Long lay the world in sin and er - ror pin - ing, till He ap - pear'd and the soul felt its worth, A thrill of hope the

O Holy Night - 2 - 1

O Holy Night - 2 - 2

O LITTLE TOWN OF BETHLEHEM

By L.H. REDNER

O Little Town Of Bethlehem - 2 - 2

ROCKIN' AROUND THE CHRISTMAS TREE

By JOHNNY MARKS

Moderato With A Rock

ROCK-IN' A-ROUND THE CHRIST-MAS TREE. at the Christ-mas par-ty hop.

Mis-tle-toe hung where you can see ev-'ry cou-ple tries to stop.

ROCK-IN' A-ROUND THE CHRIST-MAS TREE, let the Christ-mas spir-it ring.

Lat-er we'll have some pun'-kin pie and we'll do some car-ol-ing.

Rockin' Around - 2 - 1

RUDOLPH, THE RED-NOSED REINDEER

Words and Music by
JOHNNY MARKS

Rudolph, the Red-Nosed Reindeer - 3 - 1

SANTA CLAUS IS COMIN' TO TOWN

Words by
HAVEN GILLESPIE

Music by
J. FRED COOTS

Santa Claus Is Comin' to Town - 5 - 1

SILENT NIGHT

Words and Music by
JOSEPH MOHR and
FRANZ GRUBER

Silent Night - 3 - 1

Silent Night - 3 - 2

SLEIGH RIDE

Words by
MITCHELL PARISH

Music by
LEROY ANDERSON

Sleigh Ride - 3 - 1

THERE IS NO CHRISTMAS
LIKE A HOME CHRISTMAS

Words by
CARL SIGMAN

Music by
MICKEY J. ADDY

There Is No Christmas Like A Home Christmas - 2 - 1

There Is No Christmas Like A Home Christmas - 2 - 2

THIRTY-TWO FEET AND EIGHT LITTLE TAILS

(Dasher, Dancer, Prancer, Vixen, Comet, Cupid, Donner, Blitzen)

By
JOHN REDMOND, JAMES CAVANAUGH
and FRANK WELDON

Thirty-Two Feet And Eight Little Tails - 2 - 1

Thirty-Two Feet And Eight Little Tails - 2 - 2

TOYLA...

Lyric by
GLEN MacDONOUGH

by
...RBERT

THE TWELVE DAYS OF CHRISTMAS

TRADITIONAL

The Twelve Days Of Christmas - 3 - 1

The Twelve Days Of Christmas - 3 - 2

The Twelve Days Of Christmas - 3 - 3

WE WISH YOU A MERRY CHRISTMAS

TRADITIONAL ENGLISH CAROL

We Wish You A Merry Christmas - 2 - 1

We Wish You A Merry Christmas - 2 - 2

WHAT CHILD IS THIS

Words by
WILLIAM CHATTERTON DIX

Music based on "GREENSLEEVES", an
OLD ENGLISH AIR

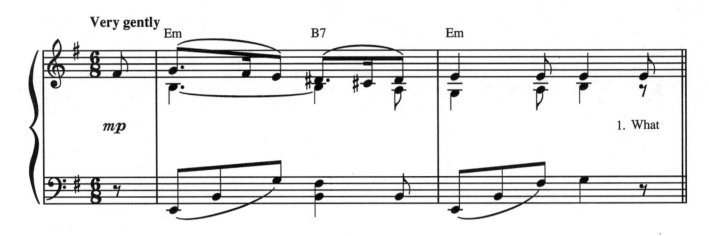

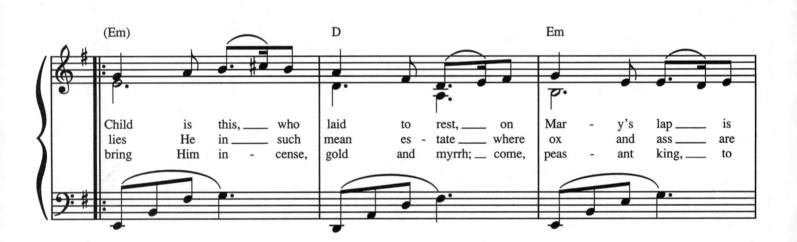

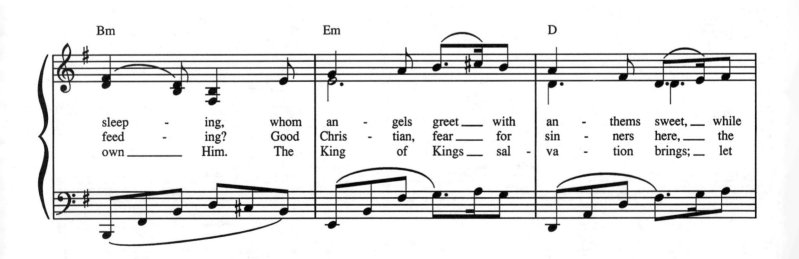

What Child Is This - 2 - 1

shep - herds watch __ are | keep _____ ing? | This, this ____ is
si - lent Word __ is | plead _____ ing. | Nails, spears __ shall
lov - ing hearts __ en - throne | Him. | Raise, raise __ the

Christ the King, __ whom | shep - herds guard __ and | an - gels sing. | Haste, haste __ to
pierce Him through __ the | cross be born, __ for | me, for you. | Hail, hail __ the
song on high; __ the | Vir - gin sings __ her | lul - a - by. | Joy, joy __ for

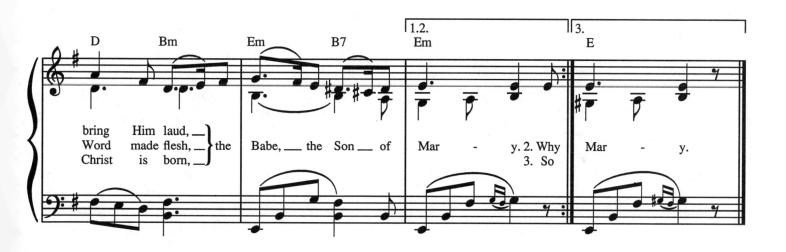

bring Him laud, __ | the Babe, __ the Son __ of | Mar - y. 2. Why | Mar - y.
Word made flesh, __ |
Christ is born, __ | | 3. So

WE THREE KINGS OF ORIENT ARE

JOHN H. HOPKINS

Showstoppers

100 or more titles in each volume of this Best-Selling Series!

Piano/Vocal/Chords:
20's, 30's, & 40's SHOWSTOPPERS
(F2865SMX)

100 nostalgic favorites include: Chattanooga Choo Choo ● Pennsylvania 6-5000 ● Blue Moon ● Moonglow ● My Blue Heaven ● Ain't Misbehavin' ● That Old Black Magic and more.

50's & 60's SHOWSTOPPERS
(F2864SMB)

Bop back to a simpler time and enjoy: Aquarius/Let the Sunshine In ● (Sittin' On) The Dock of the Bay ● Hey, Good Lookin' ● Sunny ● Johnny Angel and more.

70's & 80's SHOWSTOPPERS
P/V/C (F2863SME)
Easy Piano (F2863P2X)

100 pop songs from two decades. Titles include: Anything for You ● Blue Bayou ● Hungry Eyes ● I Wanna Dance with Somebody (Who Loves Me) ● If You Say My Eyes Are Beautiful ● I'll Never Love This Way Again ● Isn't She Lovely ● Old Time Rock & Roll ● When the Night Comes.

BIG NOTE PIANO SHOWSTOPPERS
Vol. 1 (F2871P3C)   Vol. 2 (F2918P3A)

Easy-to-read big note arrangements of 100 popular tunes include: Do You Want to Know a Secret? ● If Ever You're in My Arms Again ● Moon River ● Over the Rainbow ● Singin' in the Rain ● You Light Up My Life ● Theme from *Love Story*.

BROADWAY SHOWSTOPPERS
(F2878SMB)

100 great show tunes include: Ain't Misbehavin' ● Almost Like Being in Love ● Consider Yourself ● Give My Regards to Broadway ● Good Morning Starshine ● Mood Indigo ● Send in the Clowns ● Tomorrow.

CHRISTMAS SHOWSTOPPERS
P/V/C (F2868SMA)
Easy Piano (F2924P2X)
Big Note (F2925P3X)

100 favorite holiday songs including: Sleigh Ride ● Silver Bells ● Deck the Halls ● Have Yourself a Merry Little Christmas ● Here Comes Santa Claus ● Little Drummer Boy ● Let It Snow! Let It Snow! Let It Snow!

CLASSICAL PIANO SHOWSTOPPERS
(F2872P9X)

100 classical intermediate piano solos include: Arioso ● Bridal Chorus (from *Lohengrin*) ● Clair de Lune ● Fifth Symphony (Theme) ● Minuet in G ● Moonlight Sonata (1st Movement) ● Polovetsian Dance (from *Prince Igor*) ● The Swan ● Wedding March (from *A Midsummer Night's Dream*).

COUNTRY SHOWSTOPPERS
(F2902SMC)

A fine collection of 101 favorite country classics and standards including: Cold, Cold Heart ● For the Good Times ● I'm So Lonesome I Could Cry ● There's a Tear in My Beer ● Young Country and more.

EASY GUITAR SHOWSTOPPERS
(F2934EGA)

100 guitar arrangements of new chart hits, old favorites, classics and solid gold songs. Includes melody, chords and lyrics for songs like: Didn't We ● Love Theme from *St. Elmo's Fire* (For Just a Moment) ● Out Here on My Own ● Please Mr. Postman ● Proud Mary ● The Way He Makes Me Feel ● With You I'm Born Again ● You're the Inspiration.

EASY LISTENING SHOWSTOPPERS
(F3069SMX)

85 easy listening songs including popular favorites, standards, TV and movie selections like: After All (Love Theme from *Chances Are*) ● From a Distance ● The Greatest Love of All ● Here We Are ● Theme from *Ice Castles* (Through the Eyes of Love) ● The Vows Go Unbroken (Always True to You) ● You Are So Beautiful.

EASY ORGAN SHOWSTOPPERS
(F2873EOB)

100 great current hits and timeless standards in easy arrangements for organ include: After the Lovin' ● Always and Forever ● Come Saturday Morning ● I Just Called to Say I Love You ● Isn't She Lovely ● On the Wings of Love ● Up Where We Belong ● You Light Up My Life.

EASY PIANO SHOWSTOPPERS
Vol. 1 (F2875P2D)   Vol. 2 (F2912P2C)

100 easy piano arrangements of familiar songs include: Alfie ● Baby Elephant Walk ● Classical Gas ● Don't Cry Out Loud ● Colour My World ● The Pink Panther ● I Honestly Love You.

JAZZ SHOWSTOPPERS
(F2953SMX)

101 standard jazz tunes including: Misty ● Elmer's Tune ● Birth of the Blues ● It Don't Mean a Thing (If It Ain't Got That Swing).

MOVIE SHOWSTOPPERS
(F2866SMC)

100 songs from memorable motion pictures include: Axel F ● Up Where We Belong ● Speak Softly Love (from *The Godfather)* ● The Entertainer ● Fame ● Nine to Five ● Nobody Does It Better.

POPULAR PIANO SHOWSTOPPERS
(F2876P9B)

100 popular intermediate piano solos include: Baby Elephant Walk ● Gonna Fly Now (Theme from *Rocky)* ● The Hill Street Blues Theme ● Love Is a Many-Splendored Thing ● (Love Theme from) *Romeo and Juliet* ● Separate Lives (Love Theme from *White Nights)* ● The Shadow of Your Smile ● Theme from *The Apartment* ● Theme from *New York, New York.*

RAGTIME SHOWSTOPPERS
(F2867SMX)

These 100 original classic rags by Scott Joplin, James Scott, Joseph Lamb and other ragtime composers include: Maple Leaf Rag ● The Entertainer ● Kansas City Rag ● Ma Rag Time Baby ● The St. Louis Rag ● World's Fair Rag and many others.

ROMANTIC SHOWSTOPPERS
(F2870SMC)

101 beautiful songs including: After All (Love Theme from *Chances Are)* ● Here and Now ● I Can't Stop Loving You ● If You Say My Eyes Are Beautiful ● The Vows Go Unbroken (Always True to You) ● You Got It.

TELEVISION SHOWSTOPPERS
(F2874SMC)

103 TV themes including: Another World ● Dear John ● Hall or Nothing (The Arsenio Hall Show) ● Star Trek -The Next Generation (Main Title) ● Theme from "Cheers" (Where Everybody Knows Your Name).

The Book of Golden Series

**THE BOOK OF GOLDEN
ALL-TIME FAVORITES**
(F2939SMX) Piano/Vocal/Chords

**THE BOOK OF GOLDEN
BIG BAND FAVORITES**
(F3172SMX) Piano/Vocal/Chords

**THE BOOK OF GOLDEN
BROADWAY**
(F2986SMX) Piano/Vocal/Chords

**THE NEW BOOK OF GOLDEN
CHRISTMAS**
(F2478SMB) Piano/Vocal/Chords
(F2478EOX) Easy Organ
(F2478COX) Chord Organ

**THE BOOK OF GOLDEN
COUNTRY MUSIC**
(F2926SMA) Piano/Vocal/Chords

**THE BOOK OF GOLDEN
HAWAIIAN SONGS**
(F3113SMX) Piano/Vocal/Chords

**THE BOOK OF GOLDEN
IRISH SONGS**
(F3212SMX) Piano/Vocal/Chords

**THE BOOK OF GOLDEN
ITALIAN SONGS**
(F2907SMX) Piano/Vocal/Chords

THE BOOK OF GOLDEN JAZZ
(F3012SMX) Piano/Vocal/Chords

**THE NEW BOOK OF GOLDEN
LATIN SONGS**
(F3049SMX) Piano/Vocal/Chords

**THE NEW BOOK OF GOLDEN
LOVE SONGS**
(F2415SOX) Organ

**THE BOOK OF GOLDEN
MOTOWN SONGS**
(F3144SMX) Piano/Vocal/Chords

**THE NEW BOOK OF GOLDEN
MOVIE THEMES, Volume 1**
(F2810SMX) Piano/Vocal/Chords

**THE NEW BOOK OF GOLDEN
MOVIE THEMES, Volume 2**
(F2811SMX) Piano/Vocal/Chords

**THE BOOK OF GOLDEN
POPULAR FAVORITES**
(F2233SMX) Piano/Vocal/Chords

**THE BOOK OF GOLDEN
POPULAR PIANO SOLOS**
(F3193P9X) Intermediate/
Advanced Piano

**THE BOOK OF GOLDEN
ROCK 'N' ROLL**
(F2830SMB) Piano/Vocal/Chords

**THE NEW BOOK OF GOLDEN
WEDDING SONGS**
(F2265SMA) Piano/Vocal/Chords